MAKING A BETTER WRLD

Kids Who Make A Difference

By Gary Chandler and Kevin Graham

Twenty-First Century Books

A Division of Henry Holt and Company
New York

Twenty-First Century Books
A division of Henry Holt and Company, Inc.
115 West 18th Street
New York, New York 10011

Henry Holt® and colophon are registered trademarks of
Henry Holt and Company, Inc.
Publishers since 1866

Published in Canada by Fitzhenry & Whiteside Ltd.
195 Allstate Parkway, Markham, Ontario L3R 4T8

Printed in the United States of America on acid free paper.

Created and produced in association with Blackbirch Graphics, Inc.
Series Editor: Tanya Lee Stone

Library of Congress Cataloging-in-Publication Data

Chandler, Gary.
   Kids who make a difference / by Gary Chandler and Kevin Graham.
      p.   cm. — (Making a better world)
   Includes index.
   Summary: Focuses on some of the innovative environmental programs
that kids have founded and run.
   ISBN 0-8050-4625-9
   1. Child environmentalists—United States—Case studies—Juvenile lit-
erature. [1. Environmentalists. 2. Environmental protection. 3. Ecology.]
I. Graham, Kevin. II. Title. III. Series: Making a better world (New York,
N.Y.)
GE197.C38   1996
363.7'0525'092273—dc20   96-23067
                                                 CIP
                                                   AC

Table of Contents

Welcome to
Making a Better World

Kids of all ages are concerned about the health of our planet. Children around the world realize that their future depends on a healthy environment—one rich with a diversity of life forms and free of pollution. Many are acting on their concerns and working to improve the quality of the environment in their communities.

Others have expressed their concerns to politicians, including the president of the United States and members of the U.S. Congress. Still others are writing books and forming environmental clubs.

As the following examples show, you too can speak up and get involved in protecting the environment—you can make a difference.

All of the books in *Making a Better World* report on people—kids, parents, schools, neighborhoods, and companies—who have decided to get involved in a cause they believe in. Through their dedication, commitment, and dreams, they help to make ours a better world. Each one of the stories in this book will take you through the steps of what it took for some ordinary people to achieve something extraordinary. Of course, in the space of one book, we can share only a fraction of the wonderful stories that exist. After a long and complicated selection process, we have chosen what we believe are the most exciting subjects to tell you about.

We hope this book will encourage you to learn more about getting involved in environmental issues. Better yet, we hope all the books in this series inspire you to get involved. There are plenty of ways that each individual—including you—can make a better world. You will find some opportunities throughout this book—and there are many others out there waiting for you to discover. If you would like to write to us for more information, the address is Earth News, P.O. Box 101413, Denver, CO 80250.

Sincerely,

Gary Chandler
and
Kevin Graham

Kids Set Their Sights on Business

*T*he way a company runs its business can have a profound impact on the environment. Corporations around the world have a wide range of environmental records. Some work at minimizing negative impacts on the environment by recycling materials, producing less packaging, and developing products that help rather than hurt the environment. Others, however, seemingly don't care about their environmental record and create waste and pollute the air, soil, and water. As the stories in this chapter demonstrate, kids can speak out against irresponsible business practices and make a huge difference in how companies operate.

Anna Brown Takes the CAKE

Anna Brown has been encouraging fellow students to take action for the environment since 1989, when she was ten years old. Her enthusiasm and dedication have made a big impact.

Brown's environmental activism began on a bus ride home from school in Freeport, Maine. Several students began talking about ways they could help create a healthier future for themselves and the environment. Joined by Kirsten Nunery, Bridget Sullivan-Stevens, and Kadie York—all from George C. Soule Elementary School—Brown formed a group called Concerns About Kids' Environment (CAKE).

"Our biggest concern at the time was the trash we saw all over town," Brown says. "So we started conducting roadside and beach clean-ups to get rid of the litter."

The kids discovered that the majority of the trash was polystyrene packaging from fast-food restaurants, especially the McDonald's in Freeport. They did some research on polystyrene in order to find out more. When they realized that polystyrene is not biodegradable

In this ceremony, Robert Lyman, the superintendent of schools in Freeport, recognized CAKE for its environmental activism.

CAKE members' march down Main Street on Mother's Day led to the Freeport McDonald's ban of polystyrene packaging. (Anna Brown is shown second from right.)

(does not decompose naturally in the environment) and not made from renewable resources, the members of CAKE decided to do more than pick up the litter in their area. The group started circulating petitions in favor of a ban on polystyrene. The members carted a lot of collected trash to town-council meetings to prove their point. CAKE marched down Main Street on Mother's Day with signs that read, "Save Your Mother," meaning "Save Mother Earth." Despite opposition from the McDonald's Corporation, the Freeport Town Council passed the ban, and the Freeport McDonald's eventually cut its use of polystyrene packaging.

CAKE's work earned the founding members a trip to New York City and an appearance on NBC's "Today Show." In 1992, the group received an invitation to Washington, D.C., to meet then-senator Albert Gore. CAKE members nominated Brown to represent them on the trip, which was organized to urge the Bush administration to attend the 1992 Earth Summit in Brazil and participate in the United Nations (UN) Conference on Global Warming.

"It was really important, because if President Bush or his representatives didn't go, then why should other countries go? The United States pollutes the most," Brown comments. "We explained to Bush's aides that if he didn't shape up and act like an environmental president, then he wouldn't be re-elected."

In another CAKE effort, the members testified before the Augusta, Maine, City Council in favor of a bill that would regulate the disposal of refrigerators. They explained how coolants leak from discarded refrigerators and contribute to the destruction of the ozone layer. The group also raised $700 to help buy and preserve 14 acres of rainforest in Costa Rica.

Brown continues to be environmentally active. She spent the second half of her junior year learning about sustainable agriculture.

Brown's environmental activism earned her a spot as one of 19 young people on the Youth Advisory Board for Earth Force, which is a nonprofit U.S. organization dedicated to enabling young people everywhere to act on behalf of the Earth.

"Being a leader doesn't just mean organizing a community project," Brown explains. "Being a leader can mean thinking about your values and making your own life environmentally sustainable. Environmental actions have really set the tone for my life." She plans to pursue environmental studies in college.

Preserving Our Vital Wetlands

In 1989, a land developer in Chelmsford, Massachusetts, applied for a permit to build 180 condominiums. The developer sent notices to all the people who owned adjoining property. When Andrew Holleman and his family received one of these notices, the 12-year-old immediately turned into an environmental activist.

He couldn't believe the developer wanted to destroy the wetlands area in his neighborhood to build the condominiums. Holleman knew about the many plant and animal species living there and how the wetlands served as a floodplain to absorb water and release it slowly. He knew that the soil and plants in wetlands purify the groundwater that feeds local wells. To protect the wetland, Holleman went to the library and researched ways to stop the development.

"I found out everything about the Hatch Act, which is Massachusetts' law protecting wetlands," he says. "I also found the Town Master Plan, which had already determined that only 2.2 of the 16.3 wetlands acres there were considered solid enough to be developed."

Holleman wrote a petition describing the problem. He began circulating it to get community support to stop the issuing of a building permit for the condominium project. He also started talking to anyone who would listen. He suggested that the developer build the condominiums on the lot of an abandoned drive-in theater in the community instead.

"The developer held a community meeting to discuss the plans, and I got so many people there, it had to be held in the school gymnasium," Holleman says. "I attended meetings almost every day for ten months after that to try and build even more awareness."

He attended meetings with the conservation commission, the zoning board of appeals, and the town selectmen. Holleman would hold up the shell of a turtle he found in the wetlands in front of audiences, explaining how the development would destroy local species such as the wood turtle, blue spotted salamander, red fox, blue heron, and various hawks.

Andrew Holleman teaches his younger brother, Nick, how to identify plants.

"It wasn't exactly fun," he admits. "I enjoyed doing it, but when you've got three hours of homework to get done and have to go to a four-hour meeting and to Boy Scouts, it can get complicated."

Holleman worked alone at first, but then the community formed the Concord Road Neighborhood Association. Everyone in the area began to participate. The group raised $16,000 and hired a lawyer and an environmental scientist to help them. After ten months, the group convinced the zoning board to

11

deny the building permit for the condominiums—and the developer ended up building the project on the abandoned drive-in lot.

His efforts made Holleman an international hero. The Giraffe Project, a nonprofit organization that honors people around the world for "sticking their neck out," declared him an honorary "giraffe." In 1988 he was also the youngest recipient to receive the United Nations Environment Programme Global 500 Award. As a result, he joined other honorees in 1989 and went on a speaking tour to the Soviet Union. That year, he also addressed the UN General Assembly about the importance of environmental conservation.

Advocates for the Chesapeake

Thanks to the actions of three elementary-school students, a construction company was forced to quit dumping dirt and slurry (a mixture of rocks, soil, water, and minerals) into a small stream and clean up the damage it had already caused.

Brothers Matt and Adam Austin and their friend Chris Crecelius live in Brandywine, Maryland. Nearby is a small stream called Tom Wall's Branch. The stream feeds into a tributary of the Patuxent River, which then spills into the Chesapeake Bay.

One afternoon in 1991, the boys were playing near the stream, as they often did. But that day, they noticed that the water was gray and milky-looking and that frogs and insects were dead. "We were like, 'whoah, what happened?' It was really, really bad—in some places it was all gray and [sediment] was six inches thick," observes Matt Austin.

Maryland's environmental-education law instructs public-school environmental courses to encourage students to "make decisions and act on those decisions." The kids had just completed an ecology class at Baden Elementary School. They had learned that the dumping of chemicals, slurry, or other materials upstream posed a threat downstream as well. They had studied watershed maps and were aware that the Chesapeake Bay was threatened by all kinds of pollutants introduced into waterways upstream, including pesticides, fertilizers, oil, and sewage. Upset, the boys rounded up some friends and, with

13

All of these kids helped to protect the threatened Tom Wall's Branch. From left to right, they are: Daniel and Ryan Crecelius; Adam Austin; Chris Crecelius; Matt, Peter, and Mark Austin; and Gregory and Tara Baden.

their newfound knowledge, headed upstream to find out what had happened.

"We found a well-drilling contractor at a housing development who was dumping slurry from the drilling rig into the stream," Crecelius notes. "We asked them to quit because they were polluting the Chesapeake, but they just told us to get lost."

The three boys immediately circulated petitions throughout the area and threatened to protest publicly at the development site. They also asked their parents to call the county authorities and demand legal action. The Austin boys' father called the county's natural resources department, which then called the owner of the well-digging company.

Within hours, the owner of the company showed up at the site and made his workers stop the dumping. The county also made the company clean up the stream and stabilize the banks to prevent further erosion. The workers also had to extract sediment from the bottom of the stream by building mini-dams and using vacuum hoses to clean each segment of the stream bottom.

"Nothing can live in water that is destroyed," Crecelius concludes. "We had to do something. And we showed that a handful of young people can make a difference."

The boys prompted a film producer named Mishka Harnden to create a movie about children and the environment because he sees their efforts as "part of a groundswell movement of children all over the world becoming involved in the environment." The film was produced and shown at the 1992 Earth Summit in Brazil.

Conservation Efforts

Young people realize that actions speak louder than words. This is especially true when it comes to threats to the environment. It is helpful to talk about a problem—but just talking about it won't bring about positive change. Doing something about it—acting on a problem—is the key.

Many kids are involved with general efforts to educate and influence others to help the environment. Others are busy designing and working on projects with such specific goals as saving energy, increasing recycling, and reducing pollution. All of them know that their future is dependent on a healthy environment, and they're taking responsibility through a wide variety of actions that will help make the world a better place.

Kids Against Pollution (KAP)

When some fifth-grade students were given a homework assignment on the First Amendment to the U.S. Constitution, a New Jersey teacher unknowingly sparked an international network of child lobbyists.

In 1987, Nick Byrne, a teacher at Tenakill School in Closter, New Jersey, asked his students to analyze the news over the weekend. They were to choose an issue that they could use to exercise their freedom of speech—which is protected by the First Amendment. That weekend, the newspapers were full of stories about beach pollution. When the kids returned to class, they decided to do something about the problem. They began writing about their concerns to their state lawmakers. And about 20 of the students decided to form a club called Kids Against Pollution (KAP).

The students began encouraging their classmates to join KAP. Thanks to their hard work and determination, it now has more than 2,500 chapters in 20 countries around the world. KAP members conduct research on pollution, make speeches, and write thousands of letters to lawmakers and the media about their environmental concerns.

In the United States, national KAP members rallied behind a letter-writing campaign to the McDonald's Corporation to urge the fast-food company to stop using polystyrene packaging. In Utah, a KAP chapter played an instrumental role in closing down a toxic waste dump. In Costa Rica, a chapter is working to save rainforests.

The group's success is due to the serious way in which students research the issues and become well informed before they speak out for change. When urging its school district to switch to recycled paper, for example, the original KAP chapter in New Jersey researched figures on the district's annual paper costs. Members collected estimates from recycling companies on how much more it would cost to switch to recycled paper. The students also had a backup plan to raise the extra money for recycled paper if the district objected to the difference in cost.

KAP produces a newsletter called *Global Habitat*, which is written by and for chapter members. One of KAP's goals is to educate communities about the local toxic impact of industrial chemicals and the benefits of eliminating them, as well as to see industry replace those toxic chemicals with safer alternatives in schools, homes, and the workplace.

KAP members at work in their current head-quarters in Newport, New York.

To realize its goals, KAP encourages each chapter to seek local and state resolutions regarding the importance of an environmental bill of rights. This resolution basically declares everyone's right to clean air, land, and water. KAP members hope that this bill of rights will build awareness and support for an amendment to the U.S. Constitution at some point in the future.

KAP's influence has become truly global. Members have held speaking engagements with the United Nations, the U.S. Environmental Protection Agency, and the New York State General Assembly. The group has won numerous awards, including one from the UN Environmental Program. For their efforts, the Tenakill School KAP members also won an $85,000 computer system in a contest sponsored by IBM and *U.S. News and World Report*. This equipment will help KAP pursue its goals.

The KAP Youth Board of Directors meets to discuss the group's goals.

For More Information

Send a self-addressed, stamped envelope to Kids Against Pollution, P.O. Box 22, Newport, NY 13416, or call (315) 845-8597. The e-mail address is kap@borg.com

Saving Rare Shrimp Species

The California freshwater shrimp is endangered, and a group of schoolchildren is fighting for its life.

In 1993, a fourth-grade class in San Anselmo, California, held a discussion about endangered species. The kids were upset and motivated to get involved, so they decided to "adopt" an endangered species and do something to save it.

The kids selected the California freshwater shrimp, which is found only in 15 streams in the northern California counties of Napa, Sonoma, and Marin. The shrimp, which has been on the U.S. endangered species list since 1980, faces extinction because of the impact of creek dredging, dam building, pollution, cattle grazing, off-road all-terrain vehicles, non-native fish, and erosion.

The kids formed the Shrimp Club and began learning all they could about the shrimp. They learned that non-native fish that people have introduced into an area (for sport fishing purposes) will kill off entire populations of the shrimp. They also learned about how sensitive the shrimp is to pollution, and how the species needs willows, blackberries, and other shrubs that dip into creeks to provide it with protection and food.

The club then broke the workload down, delegating tasks such as fund raising to various committees.

"The kids have worked on creek restoration and have met with ranchers, farmers, biologists, and environmentalists," teacher Laurette Rogers says. "They have made presentations to more than 2,000 teachers, biologists, politicians, and businesspeople. They also have gone to Sacramento [the capital of California] and Washington, D.C., to lobby for the shrimp."

The students' goal is not only to save the shrimp from extinction but also to promote land stewardship, especially along the banks of the creeks where the shrimp lives. In an effort to stop the destruction of habitat around Stemple Creek from erosion, the Shrimp Club put up fencing to keep the cattle out, and in one instance, bought a bridge for cattle to cross Stemple Creek.

The kids also developed a "Shrimp Information Packet" as part of their application for the 1993 Anheuser Busch "A Pledge and a Promise" environmental-awards program. The club ended up winning the grand prize, as well as first place in its category. These awards earned the club $32,500, which provided funds to buy native plants, fencing, and a cattle bridge and for operating expenses. Other substantial grants from the

Members of the Shrimp Club study an endangered freshwater shrimp.

National Fish and Wildlife Foundation ($35,000), the Marin Community Foundation ($32,000), and the Center for Eco-literacy ($10,000) have helped the cause.

The Shrimp Club is part of a growing trend in education called "project-based learning." Students have learned about business, ecology, marine biology, environmental restoration, and political activism. They also publish an ongoing newsletter.

The Shrimp Club planted willow trees along Stemple Creek in California with rancher Paul Martin.

For More Information

Write to the Shrimp Club, Brookside School, 46 Green Valley Court, San Anselmo, CA 94960, or call (415) 454-7409.

Eco-Award Leads to Leadership Role

After William Wong won an "eco-inventors" award for designing a solar-powered car in 1993, he was invited to attend a momentous environmental gathering of youth—the Kids World Council.

The council, a project of the Children's Earth Fund and the cable-television channel Nickelodeon, involved the efforts of 56 U.S. delegates between the ages of 8 and 15. Children gathered and created a "plan for the planet"—an outline of environmental recommendations. At a meeting wrapping up the council's efforts, the delegates presented their plan to Vice-President Al Gore.

One component of the plan involved creating an "Earth force" to unify the youth environmental movement. An organization by the same name was soon formed, and Wong, a 15-year-old from San Francisco, California, was chosen to sit on the group's Youth Advisory Board.

One of the board's first decisions involved polling tens of thousands of youth to see what environmental issues concerned them the most. This was called the "Kids Choose" vote. Wong took part by talking to all the classes at his school and passing out the ballots. He later tallied all his school's ballots and sent them on to Earth Force's headquarters in Arlington, Virginia.

When the group's first campaign was chosen after the balloting, Wong again got his school involved. He persuaded many of his classmates to participate in Earth Force's 1995 Pennies for the Planet fund-raising effort, which was part of the group's first national campaign, called "Go Wild for Wildlife."

The effort raised money to help protect migratory wildlife habitats. Animals that benefited from this effort included songbirds in Guatemala, shorebirds in Argentina, sea turtles in Brazil, and humpback whales off the coast of the Dominican Republic. The campaign linked environmental education with community awareness to provide young people with an opportunity to take action on behalf of the Earth. Wong's school helped the cause by raising money through bake sales and collection buckets.

William Wong has continually made an impact with his environmental efforts.

"Earth Force campaigns help get more kids involved and informed. It shows them what needs to be done and how to participate," Wong explains. "By joining thousands of kids' efforts together, the campaigns help show them that their efforts are not in vain and taken together can have an impact.

"Our future depends on what we do," he adds. "If we want to save the environment, we hold the key. It's up to us." Earth Force's 1996 Pennies for the Planet effort, held in April, helped kids learn why trees and forests are important for a healthy planet and raised money to protect some of the world's endangered rainforests.

A Youthful Force
for the Earth

Earth Force isn't just an environmental organization *for* kids—
it is *driven* by kids. They are the ones who decide what issues
and activities the group tackles.

In fact, the organization's first effort in 1994 involved a "Kids
Choose" vote in which young people across the United States
decided what environmental issues Earth Force would address.
Ballots were distributed through a number of different avenues.
More than 145,000 kids nationwide voted overwhelmingly to
tackle wildlife as their first environmental project. The campaign
kicked off in the fall of 1994 and ran through the school year.

Called "Go Wild for Wildlife," this first national action
campaign enlisted the help of more than 200,000 young people.
Together, these volunteers pledged nearly 820,000 hours to help
wildlife and threatened habitats. Kids took hands-on actions like
building bird feeders, conducting field surveys, and cleaning
up parks and streams. They also collected more than 17.5 million pennies ($175,000) to support wildlife migratory projects.
Building from this, young people then held town meetings with
decision makers to speak out on the environmental issues they
care about.

The second campaign, held during the 1995/96 school year,
was called "Team Up for Trees!" Kids tackled issues such as
rainforest destruction and neighborhood tree-planting efforts
through actions like reducing their paper consumption, adopt-
ing local trees and planting new ones, collecting pennies for

tropical rainforest projects, and holding another series of town meetings.

To boost the effectiveness of its programs, Earth Force distributed teacher and student "action guides" free of charge. The organization charges no membership fees. Earth Force is also guided by an 18-member Youth Advisory Board. The members see the effort as a way for kids to get information, share new ideas, and put those ideas into action.

"We kids believe that if we could show every adult how beautiful the world is through our eyes, they would want to protect it," states the Youth Advisory Board. "We're working with kids across the country in action campaigns to help the environment—join the Force!"

The Youth Advisory Board for Earth Force stands in front of a tree made from recycled materials as part of the "Team Up for Trees" project.

For More Information

Write to Earth Force, 1501 Wilson Boulevard, 12th Floor, Arlington, VA 22209, or call (703) 243-7400. Visit its web site at http://www.earthforce.org/earthforce/

A Pollution Solution

(arpooling programs usually spur thoughts of businesspeople traveling downtown—not of children making their way to an elementary school. But Lara Weissblatt and her fellow classmates decided that a carpooling program for their school could help make a difference in the air quality and traffic in their town of Lauderhill, Florida.

"We matched up parents and their kids," Weissblatt explains. "About 400 people got involved, and we gave each of them a bumper sticker that said, 'Carpooling—The Pollution Solution.' Parents love it. There's less traffic at drop-off and pick-up, and they don't have to drive so often." Through the carpooling effort, the students took on new projects. Eventually, they started a group called Florida Kids for Clean Air. The group's members conducted and participated in beach clean-ups and visited classrooms to pass out information and talk about air-pollution problems and possible solutions.

The carpooling program is still under way, although Weissblatt and

Weissblatt and other kids plant a tree with Lauderhill's Mayor Ilene Lieberman on Arbor Day.

her classmates now attend Nova Middle School. One of Weissblatt's key role models, however, was Charlotte Pine, a teacher at her elementary school. Pine sparked her interest in the environment by presenting issues such as deforestation, air pollution, and global warming to the students.

Weissblatt participated in the Kids World Council, which is an international gathering of youth representatives. She was invited after winning an essay contest about her plan to help improve the environment. In 1996, Weissblatt made another environmental contribution by speaking her mind at a city-council meeting. She was honored at the meeting for being a part of the Kids World Council.

Lara Weissblatt helped to establish Florida Kids for Clean Air in a successful effort to improve air quality by getting people to carpool.

"After talking about Kids World Council, I told the city council that it should expand its recycling program to include a lot more trash—like juice boxes, colored glass, paper milk cartons, and more types of plastic," Weissblatt says. "A few weeks later, they sent me a letter saying they were going to do it! I felt like I had accomplished something."

Weissblatt knows that she helps to make a difference in the environment, but she is still concerned about the future.

"If we don't start doing something about the environment now, there will be no future for us," she explains. "The adults are ruining it and just passing the burden on to us. I know

27

Lara Weissblatt and her sister raised money to benefit the "Go Wild for Wildlife" project.

there are a lot of environmental groups with adults involved that are trying to do something, but we still have a long way to go, and kids can help."

In one project organized by Weissblatt, a fund-raising effort was done to help Earth Force's "Go Wild for Wildlife" campaign. In another project undertaken by Florida Kids for Clean Air, the group raised more than $600 to buy rainforest land in Costa Rica. The group raised the money by selling rainforest-related items, such as notepads with sayings like, "If a toucan can, you can too—save the rainforest." They also sold Tree Tops—blow pops that were covered with green tissue paper tied with brown string.

For her environmental activism, Weissblatt was chosen to be a member of the Earth Force Youth Advisory Board. "My message to kids across the United States is to remember that they have the power to change the world," Weissblatt comments.

Spreading the Word

Many of today's young people believe that ignorance—being uninformed on an issue—poses a great threat to the environment. And many kids have learned that education is the foundation for positive change in the world.

To minimize the effects of ignorance, they have tackled environmental projects of all types around the world. These include explaining the importance of diversity of plant and animal life—called biodiversity—and the strains caused by expanding human populations.

Since kids' futures depend on the environment, they have the most to lose if the environment is not protected. They can help to spread the word to make sure we are all doing our part to conserve and recycle. Our health and well-being depend on it.

Youth Say YES!
to the Environment

Ryan Eliason wasn't the first teenager to dream about changing the world, but he was quick to turn his dreams into action.

In 1990, at the age of 19, Eliason and his 16-year-old friend Ocean Robbins founded an international organization called Youth for Environmental Sanity (YES!). YES! is run by young people and is a project of the nonprofit EarthSave International. Its mission is to inform, inspire, and empower youth to make a difference through school-assembly presentations, workshops, and summer camps. On a YES! speaking tour, members talk to junior-high-school and high-school students about the environmental aspects of many issues, such as energy, food, water, and recycling.

"We talk about the environmental crisis and about choices," one of the original members, Sol Solomon, explains. "We talk about what young people can do to make a difference."

After YES! speakers leave a school, students typically begin taking action. One group of students got its school district to ban Styrofoam. Another got its school store to sell only recycled paper products. Yet another group began organizing clean-ups of the school grounds. Some got their schools to start composting, while several even organized regional speaking tours to spread the YES! messages.

One of the messages promoted by YES! concerns the interdependence of all life forms on Earth and the health problems caused by pollution. Water pollution is also a serious problem addressed. YES! teaches that we can do much to save the clean water we have and to keep it from being contaminated through the choices we make with our food, energy, and trash.

Since 1991, YES! has run 24 summer camps for youth throughout the United States, as well as in Australia, New Zealand, Singapore, Taiwan, Costa Rica, and Canada. Camp participants learn skills of community organizing, leadership, communication, obtaining media coverage, and public speaking.

In addition, Solomon has been the primary organizer of the World Youth Leadership Camp, which brings together youth and adult environmentalists from around the world for a week of learning. The program marks the beginning of an exciting global network of youth activists.

Another program the organization promotes is called the Green Schools Energy Project, which shows school systems how to save money on energy through more efficient design and lights. In Santa Cruz, California, the schools now collectively save $160,000 per year on energy costs. Along with saving natural resources and reducing pollution, this effort puts that money into educational programs.

YES! reaches more than 100,000 students through its programs every year. In addition, Solomon and Robbins have written a book called *Choices for Our Future, A Generation Rising for Life On Earth*. The group has received financial help from different organizations. They have been sponsored by Greenpeace, Aveda, Esprit, Human-i-Tees, and others.

YES! members travel to schools around the world spreading their message of environmental awareness. (Sol Solomon is shown second from left and Ocean Robbins fourth from left, both in the back row.)

For More Information

Write to YES!, 706 Frederick Street, Santa Cruz, CA 95062, or call (408) 459-9344. You can also e-mail it at yes@cruzio.com

Essay Contest Inspires
Young Environmentalist

Chris DiNero thinks that ignorance is the greatest threat to the environment, so he's been working to educate world leaders about environmental problems since he was 11 years old.

DiNero's involvement began when Susan LeBeau, his fifth-grade teacher at West End Elementary School in Long Branch, New Jersey, received a lesson packet from the Children's Earth Fund. Since she teaches about the environment, LeBeau felt that her students should respond to the essay contest about global warming included in the packet.

DiNero was one of two national winners in this competition, called "Beat the Heat." The other winner was Erica Martinez, 11, of San Antonio, Texas. They each won a trip to Washington, D.C., in January 1992.

DiNero and Martinez joined 16 other kids from various U.S. youth environmental organizations to deliver 100,000 petitions to then-president George Bush. The petitions demanded that the United States reduce its carbon dioxide (CO_2) emissions by 20 percent by the year 2000. The petitions were part of the CO_2 Challenge, in which 200,000 children pledged to reduce CO_2 emissions by 400 million pounds through energy conservation efforts. The petitions declared, "We, the environment generation, say no to CO_2. Carbon dioxide from burning fossil fuels is the primary source of global warming. We [the United States] have only 5 percent of the world's population, yet we produce 25 percent of the world's CO_2."

A few months later, DiNero carried the global-warming message to the United Nations. During a UN General Assembly preparation event for the Earth Summit, held in Brazil in July 1992, he described the group's hopes for a worldwide effort to stop global warming.

As impressive as these efforts are, DiNero doesn't consider any of these as his greatest environmental accomplishment. He says that serving on the Youth Advisory Board of Earth Force ranks at the top. "One person can only do so much," DiNero says. "Through Earth Force, I'm able to touch thousands of young lives, and they go on and make a bigger difference."

DiNero wrote a news column for a major daily newspaper in New Jersey, and he's helping to start an on-line computer project to help link his fellow Earth Force members. He also chaired the Kids World Council in 1992. International participants from around the world gathered to discuss environmental issues with leaders such as U.S. vice-president Al Gore. The sponsor, Nickelodeon, then broadcast the resulting three-hour television program numerous times.

"The Kids World Council was so much fun," DiNero says. "People from South America, Europe, Africa, and Asia came together for three days to talk about the environment." He adds, "It's interesting how the social environments from around the world are so different, but the environmental concerns are so similar."

Chris DiNero gives a "thumbs up" for environmental activism.

Planting Peace

Tim Mack, a high-school student in Connecticut, along with two other Natural Guard members Joseph Golden and Shunte Corley, have come up with a unique idea that ties environmental awareness with the social problem of youth violence.

"In New Haven, we have a lot of shootings," he notes. "All these kids are dying over nothing, and I thought that maybe I could make a difference. For every kid who dies, we ask the parents' permission to plant a memorial tree along with a plaque that describes the person who died."

Each plaque lists the victim's name, birth and death dates, and explains how the person died. The plaque also includes a message from the parents of the child and a thank-you note to the parents for taking part in the effort.

So far, about a dozen trees and plaques have been placed along a bike trail in New Haven, and the idea is receiving a lot of positive responses. Mack now hopes to create a larger plaque to describe the project to bike-trail users.

The project is one of many that Mack has taken part in as a member of a group called the Natural Guard. The efforts of this nonprofit organization help young people learn more about the environment and what they can do to protect it.

A book is another project being tackled by Mack's New Haven chapter of the Natural Guard. Called *In My Backyard*, the book grew out of correspondence kids sent to the group.

"We kept getting letters from kids asking us things like how to start a garden, how to plant a tree, how to organize a beach clean-up, as well as wanting information about animals and so on," Mack says. "So we decided to answer all their

Tim Mack has found a way to promote peace and help the environment in the city by planting trees in memory of lost youth.

questions in a book. We've written more than 100 pages over the last year and a half."

Mack is a student at the Sound Magnet School, where he enjoys studying marine biology. When asked to describe the future of the environment, Mack explains that he is not sure. "At this point, I think we're in trouble," he says. "But kids have a better chance of saving the Earth than adults because we will work together.

"Right now, I'd say we have about two thirds of the youth on board. We need the other third to join us; then we can force the adults to help. If we make up our minds, we will get it done, but we need more involvement so we can all live in a better place in the future."

The Natural Guard

Richie Havens founded the Natural Guard to empower inner-city children to effect change.

To many people, violence in the street is not an environmental issue. However, to the Natural Guard, it is. The youth-education organization believes that all of society's problems are environmental in nature.

"We define our environment as the place where we live, and for many children that includes threats from lead poisoning both inside and outside their homes, contaminated needles in urban parks, and violence in the streets," says Diana Edmonds, who is the executive vice-chair of the group.

The Natural Guard considers itself to be part of the environmental-justice movement. This links environmental concerns with social issues like unemployment, lack of opportunity for poor families, and the disproportionate impact of environmental degradation on people of color.

The group was founded by musician Richie Havens in New Haven, Connecticut, in 1990, and now has kids involved in the program from nine of the city's schools, including two elementary schools, five junior-high schools, and three high schools.

Natural Guard chapters have also sprung up in New Jersey, Pennsylvania, New York, and Hawaii. The group even has two chapters in Belize, in Central America. A total of 1,700 young people are involved. The Natural Guard is open to all young people, free of charge.

"Our goal is to empower youth to see their local communities as the environment most in need of their stewardship," Edmonds explains. "We then assist them with the tools and mentors they need to address the community's various problems."

The Natural Guard in New Haven has developed a program for area youth to explore ecosystems linked to Long Island Sound. With access to a sailing vessel owned by a local environmental organization called Schooner, Inc., the Natural Guard takes members on field trips to study water quality and collect specimens. By understanding ecosystems, people are better prepared to protect them.

Natural Guard members set out on an expedition to study a marine ecosystem.

Also in New Haven, the Natural Guard was able to secure four plots of land through the New Haven Land Trust to use as urban gardens. The organization plants and harvests a variety of fruits and vegetables, donating 80 percent of the produce to community soup kitchens. The Natural Guard is conducting an inventory of blighted properties and streets in New Haven that are in need of trees. The group's efforts already have led

A community garden is being readied for planting by The Natural Guard.

Connecticut's Department of Environmental Protection to clean up 30 illegal dumping sites.

The members of the chapters in Belize are gathering mahogany seeds and have already planted and begun to raise 1,500 trees in a nursery. The Belize government has since contracted with the group to grow another 2,500 trees.

"The Natural Guard is a multicultural group that helps the environment by offering youth involvement to communities by affirming their ownership of the local environment," Edmonds says. "In turn, the youth educate the broader environmental community of various urban and public-health issues that need addressing."

For More Information

Write to the Natural Guard, 142 Howard Avenue, New Haven, CT 06519, or call (203) 787-0229.

Children's Alliance Empowers Youth

A unique conservation organization that succeeded at giving children a loud voice for several years taught them that effecting a difference in the health of the environment is an effort worth making.

"Our mission was to change environmental attitudes and behavior through responsible conservation and restoration activities of young people around the world," says Ingrid Kavanagh, founder and president of the Children's Alliance for Protection of the Environment (CAPE).

Environmental literacy was the backbone of the program. The nonprofit group produced several publications and educational programs. These were distributed to children, schools, and clubs in 35 countries. A quarterly newspaper was written by student members who submitted articles from around the world. And the alliance produced a bimonthly newsletter for adult supporters and a separate newsletter for teachers.

In addition, CAPE prepared a Program Guide, a 140-page action-oriented guide that assisted teachers and adults in promoting responsible action by children. The group also wrote a biweekly column for a daily newspaper in Austin, Texas.

"We received letters every day from children expressing their anxiety and asking for information about how they can help protect the environment," Kavanagh explains. "Their concern and sincere desire to take action were the driving forces behind CAPE."

CAPE members hike through the Children's Forest that was created due to CAPE's efforts.

CAPE has led efforts to clean up beaches, lakeshores, and riverbanks in Turkey, Zimbabwe, Romania, and Argentina. Kavanagh traveled to still more countries to lead other clean-up efforts and to give presentations. "CAPE was a catalyst for environmental education and action," she says. "I guess we were crusaders."

As a result of its hard work, CAPE was honored by the United Nations Environment Programme (UNEP) and was a member of the program's Global 500 Roll of Honor. Kavanagh also served as UNEP's regional youth advisor for the United States. CAPE's other accomplishments include the establishment of a "Children's Forest" near Austin and the preservation of more than 2,500 acres of rainforest in Costa Rica.

The alliance started without any operating money and relied on grants and donations to survive. The group was technically a membership organization, but children weren't charged a fee. "We didn't want economic factors to restrict the flow of information to kids," Kavanagh explains. "Since we sent so much information to schools, though, we asked them to pay a $100 annual membership fee when possible." Due to lack of funding, Earth Force now helps administer CAPE.

Mother Turns Daughter
Into Activist

Courtney Collins didn't really want to go to the children's environmental meeting in Austin, Texas, but her mother didn't give her a choice. As it turned out, however, the ten-year-old enjoyed it so much that she quickly became an international environmental leader.

The meeting was the first organizing meeting for CAPE. After the meeting, her childhood changed forever.

Collins immediately became very good friends with the founder of CAPE, Ingrid Kavanagh. Collins's school, Casis Elementary, became the first CAPE chapter school in the country. Kavanagh and Collins went to other schools and gave lectures and workshops about environmental issues. They also organized such activities as beach clean-ups and trash pickups around schools and towns.

"That's what CAPE was for—to inform other children on how to help the environment," Collins says. "I taught children my age and younger that helping the environment is something we have to do and that it isn't that hard to do."

Collins went to Mexico City with CAPE to accept the group's Global 500 Award, given by the United Nations Environment Programme in 1992.

"I met kids from all over the world, and it gave me a lot of hope and a real sense of accomplishment. We all had one common goal, and we were all working together. Even though we're totally foreign to each other, it didn't matter because we're

*In January 1992,
Courtney Collins
spoke at a U.S.
Senate panel
hearing regard-
ing reducing
CO$_2$ emissions
through energy
conservation.*

kids," she says. "Politics didn't matter to us. I realized there was hope." In 1994, at age 15, Collins joined the Earth Force Youth Advisory Board.

In the fall of 1995, Collins put on a workshop at the UN Youth Environmental Summit. The workshop was about conservation, preservation, and restoration. "We're telling kids that the three concepts really coincide with each other," she said. "If you do one, you have to try to do the others."

Collins is still involved with Earth Force, as that organization has stepped in to help CAPE through some financial difficulties. Collins has taken what she learned with CAPE and applies it to her other activities. She still makes presentations at local schools and gives the kids projects to do.

"Ignorance can destroy the environment," she explains. "If we don't do something now, we won't be able to do anything later."

The Tree Musketeers

After a group of eight-year-old girls was forced to use paper plates on a camping trip, they were inspired to plant their first tree and ended up creating an award-winning conservation organization.

In 1987, Tara Church's Brownie troop from El Segundo, California, held a meeting to plan its trip to the Southern California Diamond Jubilee Roundup, a gathering of more than 15,000 girls. Because of a lack of water at their camping site, organizers urged the attendees to break with Girl Scout camping standards and use disposable dishes.

Initially, the girls were given the choice of washing dishes or using disposable ones, so the troop leaders presented the pros and cons of each option. When the girls learned the connection between paper plates and trees—and heard how the plates would contribute to landfill problems— they decided to walk the extra mile to reach water to wash their dishes. Unfortunately, later the troop was informed that paper plates were the only option.

"Before we went home, we planted a sycamore tree to help make up for the damage we and the other campers would do to the environment on that trip," Church says. "We called her Marcie the Marvelous Tree. It

Tara Church welcomes delegates to the first National Youth Environmental Summit in 1993.

The Tree Musketeers "Homeless Baby Tree Adoptions" program allows kids to nurture baby trees into adulthood.

taught us what people can accomplish by planting trees, and it gave us a sense of power that we didn't have before."

The girls proceeded to start Tree Musketeers—an organization staffed and run by kids. The group aimed to help the environment through its own efforts and by challenging young people and businesses to join the environmental movement. One of the group's first goals involved planting a protective ring of trees around the entire town of El Segundo, which is surrounded by the noise and pollution of large industries. Tree Musketeers has since planted more than 1,000 trees in El Segundo, and, through its "Homeless Baby Tree Adoptions" program, thousands of other seedlings have been distributed.

Church and the other co-founders are now out of high school, but they have an impressive list of accomplishments behind them. Among other things, the group started El Segundo's first complete recycling center, reducing the city's residential waste by 16 percent within the first 4 months. Tree Musketeers also presents annual awards to citizens and businesses for environmental efforts.

Tara Church accepts the President's Volunteer Action Award from Bill Clinton.

The group's efforts earned it the 1988 National President's Environmental Youth Award. In 1989, the Musketeers won a National Arbor Day Foundation Award. And President Bill Clinton gave Tree Musketeers the President's Volunteer Action Award in 1994.

In 1993, the group organized the first National Youth Environmental Summit in Cincinnati, Ohio. The event brought hundreds of organizations together for four days to discuss ways to reverse the damage that humans have done to the Earth. The group held its second summit in Snowbird, Utah, in 1995; one of the few rules for the summit was that all adults had to be accompanied by a young person.

For More Information

Write to Tree Musketeers, 136 Main Street, El Segundo, CA 90245-3800, or call (310) 322-0263.

Doing Double Duty

A teacher in Seattle has encouraged students all over North America to help wipe out environmental ignorance—one grocery bag at a time.

Earth Day Groceries is a project started in 1994 by Mark Ahlness, a third-grade teacher at Arbor Heights Elementary School in Seattle, Washington. He gathered grocery bags from local stores and brought them to school for "environmental decoration." The idea caught on quickly. After students put drawings of wildlife and the Earth on the bags, as well as added their own statements about conservation and recycling, the bags were returned to the stores and filled with customers' groceries. Pretty soon students at other schools were getting involved. Schools now send Ahlness reports concerning how many bags have been decorated and distributed. By 1996, nearly 70,000 students around the country were getting their messages of environmental awareness out to consumers.

"I put an invitation out over the Internet encouraging other schools to join us. There were 43 schools involved the first year, 115 the second, and 177 in 1996," he says. "It's a great environmental-education tool for the students and the public. People in the neighborhood find out that there are many kids in the area who care—and care enough to spread the word. I think it's making a difference."

Ahlness came across the idea a few years before at a conference for teachers. Most of the students do the project as part of their environmental-education classes or ecology clubs. Elementary schools are the main participants, but some junior-high schools and high schools are also involved.

"Our school was one of the very first in the country to have its own web site," Ahlness says. "Schools find our home page and then just get involved on their own. I'm always getting information from someone who participated last year and decided to file a report."

White Plains Middle School in New York wrote Ahlness the following:

"Thanks so much for the idea! Our entire sixth grade decorated a total of 600 bags for two different grocery stores. We also included special-education students in the project. It was exciting going to the stores on Earth Day and helping bag groceries with our bags. The students who went on this trip also got to fill out job applications."

Ahlness says that people don't have to sign up for the project or register. He urges students and teachers alike to have a great time and send in brief reports with counts of the number of bags each school designs and distributes. Reports can be filed via e-mail. Be sure to include the name of your school or club, as well as the town. Also indicate if you would like to receive, via e-mail, all the reports from other schools.

This is one of thousands of illustrated grocery bags that were made by students in order to heighten environmental awareness by consumers.

For More Information

Use the e-mail address: mahlness@cks.ssd.k12.wa.us You can also visit the home page at: http://www.halcyon.com/arborhts/earth-day.html Be sure to look into the file labeled "Frequently Asked Questions."

Influencing Lawmakers for Change

Throughout the world, local and national lawmakers are in positions to create and influence environmental laws and regulations. It is their job to represent the goals of the people in their communities. In turn, young people can influence the policies and other decisions that these legislators make. In fact, to see a law or policy changed, environmental activists usually need to work with their local lawmakers and other government officials at some point.

Kids may not be old enough to vote, but they are old enough to speak their minds and communicate their concerns about the environment. They can start by getting their parents' support. After talking with them, kids can find ways to get the attention and support of others.

Kids F.A.C.E.® the Future

Teenager Melissa Poe didn't set out to change the world, but her efforts might end up having that effect.

In 1989, when she was nine years old, Poe saw an episode of the late Michael Landon's "Highway to Heaven" television show. The program depicted what the world's environment might look like in 20 years. Pollution was everywhere, and ecosystems were in shambles. The images frightened Poe.

"In 20 years, I'd be almost 30 years old," she explains. "So I sat down that night and wrote a letter to the president, asking that something be done."

When she didn't receive a timely response from then-president George Bush, Poe set in motion a media campaign to make her point that the environment is important to the future of civilization. That effort ended up bringing her fame and resulted in a far-reaching environmental effort.

First, Poe called several outdoor-advertising companies and asked about a possible donation of free billboard space. Soon her letter to Bush filled a billboard in Washington, D.C., along with one in her hometown of Nashville, Tennessee. It read: "Dear Mr. President: Please will you do something about pollution. I want to live until I am a 100 years old. Mr. President, if you ignore this letter we will all die of pollution. Please help!"

Twelve weeks later, Poe received a response to her letter, but it was not what she had expected from the president of the United States. The reply was simply a standard form letter, asking her to stay in school and not to use drugs.

Poe placed a call to the Outdoor Advertising Association of America that spurred the organization to feature Poe's letter

Dear Mr. President,
Please will you do something about pollution. I want to live till I am a 100 years old. Mr. President, if you ignore this letter We will all die of pollution.
Please Help! Melissa Poe, Age 9 Nashville, Tennessee

Reagan

Melissa Poe's plea for environmental awareness displayed on this billboard was the beginning of Kids F.A.C.E.®

on 250 billboards across the nation. After appearing on NBC's "Today Show" and talking about President Bush's response, a second letter from the president soon followed, saying that he regretted not answering her concerns in the first letter.

As Poe got more and more media attention, other children started calling her. They wanted to know what they could do to help. She decided to start a club—called Kids For A Clean Environment (Kids F.A.C.E.®)—to help children get involved in environmental activities and form groups in their schools. Kids F.A.C.E.® now has more than 200,000 members. They undertake tree-planting and recycling projects, as well as other efforts, and help create awareness about the environment among their classmates and parents.

When expenses for the club—for such things as postage and long-distance phone calls—grew too large for her family to handle, Poe again relied on her youthful initiative. She wrote a letter to the giant retail-store chain Wal-Mart, asking for help. Sam Walton, the founder of Wal-Mart, wrote back and offered to pay for a bimonthly newsletter for Kids F.A.C.E.® as well as all related postage.

Poe now sends material for each newsletter to Wal-Mart, which designs, prints, and mails it to all the club's members. Material for the publication comes from the more than 200 letters Poe receives every day, most filled with thoughts, ideas, and poems about the environment.

For her efforts, Poe has become a celebrity of sorts. She was flown out to California to meet Michael Landon and has been featured in a Wal-Mart television advertisement. During a 1995 Earth Day event in Washington, D.C., she spoke in front of more than 100,000 people.

While in the nation's capital, Poe and some of her fellow Kids F.A.C.E.® members unfurled a huge flag the club had created, composed of 20,000 individual drawings. The founder

Poe addresses an Earth Day crowd in Washington, D.C., and accepts an award for Kids F.A.C.E.® efforts.

of Earth Day, Gaylord Nelson, spoke at the flag's unveiling on the Washington Mall, and a letter from Vice-President Al Gore was read to the crowd.

The idea for the flag came from a project that Poe had initiated for her school's Kids F.A.C.E.® chapter. The chapter wanted a piece of artwork for its T-shirts, so each member created a drawing on a 12-inch-square piece of cloth. "We used markers or paints and drew what we thought the world should look like, or animals or something involving the Earth," Poe says. "Then we picked out our favorite for the T-shirts. But we didn't want the other drawings to go to waste, so we decided to start making a flag."

With 20 drawings now composing the Kids F.A.C.E.® flag, the group decided to turn the project into a large-scale effort. Letters from the chapter about the flag soon spurred articles in periodicals such as *Seventeen*, *Weekly Reader*, and *Scholastic Magazine*. The Kids F.A.C.E.® newsletter also trumpeted the effort. Over the next year, 5,000 cloth squares arrived from around the world at the Kids F.A.C.E.® chapter headquarters in Nashville, each carefully created by children. The squares featured sayings such as "Help save the Earth," poems, song lyrics, or hand-drawn pictures of eagles, trees, or other environmental images.

When a final call for squares went out in the club's newsletter early in 1995—along with infor-mation about dedicating the flag on Earth Day in Washington—yard after yard of material soon started to arrive at Poe's doorstep. More than 15,000 decorated squares tripled the size of the club's flag in just over three months. Poe, her mother, and many other volunteers had plenty of sewing to do in order to meet their Earth Day deadline. "I was amazed at how big it became," Poe exclaims. "It was exciting to watch it grow bigger and bigger."

In one of her many environ-mental activities, Poe participates in a tree-planting project.

By Earth Day, the flag measured 100 by 200 feet. More cloth squares continued to arrive after the dedication ceremony, and Poe says that the flag—along with its overall mission to involve children in environmental activities—will continue to grow. "Kids F.A.C.E.® is there to get kids involved in helping the environment," Poe says. "I hope people start to realize that kids can make a difference when they put their minds to it. One day, hopefully the environment will be OK, and we won't have to worry about it anymore."

For More Information

Write to Kids F.A.C.E.®, P.O. Box 158254, Nashville, TN 37215, or call (800) 952-FACE.

Speaking Role Leads to Environmental Action

When John Hegstrand was 12, his speaking skills landed him a big role in New York City. No, the part wasn't on Broadway. It involved giving a nearly 20-minute presentation in front of a huge audience in the United Nations' General Assembly Hall.

Hegstrand, of Plymouth, Minnesota, had been chosen to take part in the United Nations' 1990 Youth Environmental Forum. He was picked to give the presentation after competing with fellow students in a speech-giving contest.

As a founding member of Kids for Saving Earth (KSE), an environmental group at his elementary school, Hegstrand already had an interest in environmental issues. The UN forum gave him a chance to act further on that interest.

John Hegstrand gets a hand from Vice-President Al Gore during the CO$_2$ Challenge event in 1990 (discussed on page 32).

54

Hegstrand and other KSE members attending the forum also had attached pledges signed by kids under each of the seats in the UN assembly hall. Each child had pledged to try and protect the environment.

"At one point, we had everyone look under their seats and hold up the pledges to demonstrate just how many kids are concerned about the future of the environment," Hegstrand says.

With help from Target, a chain of retail stores, Hegstrand's presentation about KSE was also a big hit back home. "Target helped us set up a satellite hook-up back to downtown Minneapolis [Minnesota]," he explains. "There we had 200 orchestra musicians playing the KSE theme song."

Two years later, in 1992, Hegstrand attended the Earth Summit in Brazil at the request of Voice of the Children, an international environmental youth organization based in Norway. There he attended the Children's Hearing along with 20 young people from other countries. They talked about what other U.S. children were doing to help the environment.

Hegstrand (left) continues his environmental activism as a member of Earth Force's Youth Advisory Board.

"I wanted to let people know that children from the United States were concerned about the environment, despite the [negative] actions by the U.S. government at the Summit," he says.

Today, Hegstrand is still concerned about the environment. "The biggest problem is ignorance. Too many people still don't think that there's anything wrong with the environment," he comments. "They need to realize that there are real problems that need to be addressed. More education is what is needed. People need to hear things over and over, and if it comes from kids, it has a bigger impact."

Although Kids for Saving Earth disbanded two years ago because of financial problems, the group once had 300,000 children involved in environmental efforts.

Students Truly "Make A Difference"

An award-winning educational program that combines social studies, civics, and environmentalism has increased students' awareness and involvement dramatically.

"Make A Difference" is an educational program developed in 1986 by Alan Haskvitz, an eighth-grade teacher at Suzanne Middle School in Walnut, California.

Through this program, students have succeeded at simplifying their county's voter instructions and getting their proposed modifications adopted by the local government. They have also translated city recycling rules into numerous languages so that new immigrants can understand how to participate.

One of the students' most notable accomplishments began when they identified water conservation as one area in which they might be able to make a difference in the environment. The students began writing laws to require state buildings to use water-saving plants in landscaping.

They spent vast amounts of time in the library conducting research on California's constant political battles over water distribution. Then they began scheduling guest speakers for their class. Landscape specialists came and explained the benefits and options involved with xeriscaping—using drought-resistant plants that need little or no water to live. The students then planted their own xeriscape garden next to their classroom to study this alternative further.

"The students devised a plan to gather statewide support for the water-saving legislation [laws] they were writing," Haskvitz notes. "They never even considered failure."

As a result of the kids' work with government officials, lobbyists, and the press, the California Senate passed the students' legislation as a resolution that should voluntarily be adhered to by all managers of state buildings.

Suzanne Middle School students participate in a garden project.

In 1996, the students decided to tackle the problem of mass balloon releases that occur regularly at various events. These balloons, released by the thousands, often end up being swallowed by sea turtles, which mistake their flimsy remains as food. In addition, the balloons are an unnecessary form of pollution dotting the land and sea.

"The students invited the lobbyists from the balloon industry to a debate," Haskvitz says. "The debate was conducted in public in front of a judge. When it was over, the students won the debate."

Although the students are having a tough time getting laws approved to ban the massive releases, they have been successful on other counts. For instance, they wrote to the Guinness Book of World Records asking them to discontinue recognizing such records as the most balloons released by an individual or organization. Guinness agreed and no longer publishes that information. This has prevented the frivolous mass release of balloons around the world. Disneyland and other organizations have also pledged to quit the controversial practice.

For More Information

A book of resources and contacts for this program is available through Alan Haskvitz, 9655 Carrari Court, Alta Loma, CA 91737.

Give Each Other a Hand

You can help increase environmental awareness by identifying the people in your school or community who have done important things on behalf of a healthy environment. Write a letter to the editor or publisher of your local newspaper explaining what the environmental activists did and why their actions are important and noteworthy. Urge the newspaper to write a story about these people.

Be sure to cover all of the following key points in your letter and follow-up telephone calls: who the people are; what they did; why they did it; why it is important to the community; how they accomplished the effort; and when and where the actions took place. This type of positive recognition can inspire others to get involved while drawing attention to the importance of environmental issues.

You could also create an award program at your school or in your community that recognizes people for doing positive things. This type of recognition encourages other people to get involved in helping the environment. Before you know it, several more people will be inspired to get involved in environmental activities.

The award program can simply involve choosing an environmental leader of the week or month and putting winners' names and photographs up on the school bulletin board or announcing their names over the public address system. You might also submit winning names and stories to your local news media in the form of a press release to try and create a bigger impact.

Glossary

biodegradable Something that decomposes naturally.

biodiversity The combined diversity of plant and animal species on Earth.

chapter A local branch of a club or organization.

conservation The preservation or protection of a natural resource.

ecology The science that deals with how living things relate to their environment and to each other.

endangered species A species that is in immediate danger of extinction.

First Amendment The freedom of speech granted to all American citizens under the U.S. Constitution.

floodplain A plain located along a river that is created by deposits of soil from floodwaters.

global warming When carbon dioxide accumulates in the Earth's atmosphere and acts like a layer of insulation, preventing the Earth's heat from escaping to higher elevations where it can cool and return back down in a continual air-and-temperature exchange.

groundwater Water that has flowed or seeped beneath the surface of the earth. It is the source of water for underground springs and wells.

habitat The place where a plant or animal naturally lives and grows.

ignorance When a person has not been exposed to certain information.

landfill Trash disposal that involves burying garbage in the ground; a landfill is often a huge pit in the ground.

land stewardship The management and protection of a piece of land.

lobby An attempt by an individual or group to get public officials to vote or respond in a particular way.

non-native species When a species exists in an area because it was introduced there by humans.

nonprofit organization An organization that exists to provide a social or other purpose and that does not strive to generate profits for owners.

nonrenewable resource A resource that can be used up, or a resource that is finite. Oil and coal are nonrenewable resources.

nursery A place where plants and trees are grown for eventual transplanting.

ozone layer An atmospheric layer about 20 to 30 miles above the Earth composed of high ozone (O_3) content. The layer helps screen out harmful ultraviolet rays from reaching the Earth's surface.

pesticides Chemicals that are used to destroy plants or animals.

petition A document that demands change and is signed by as many individuals as possible who want a government or organization to change a policy or practice.

polystyrene A rigid transparent thermoplastic found in molded products, foams, and sheet materials.

renewable resource A resource that occurs naturally and is theoretically inexhaustible, such as wind.

restoration The act of restoring something to its former state or condition.

sanity The ability to make rational decisions.

slurry A mixture of water, rocks, soil, and minerals.

sustainable A practice that can be done in an unlimited manner because of the minimal impact it has on the environment.

toxic Having the effect of a poison.

tributary A stream or river that flows into a larger body of water.

watershed The natural contours of the land through which rain and snowmelt drain.

wetlands Areas of land such as swamps and tidal flats that typically contain a high content of moisture in the soil.

xeriscaping Landscaping with drought-resistant plants.

Further Reading

Earth Works Group Staff. *Kid Heroes of the Environment: Simple Things Real Kids Are Doing to Save the Earth.* Berkeley, CA: Earth Works, 1991.

Gardner, Robert. *Experimenting with Energy Conservation.* Danbury, CT: Watts, 1992.

Gutnik, Martin J. *Recycling: Learning the Four R's: Reduce, Reuse, Recycle, Recover.* Springfield, NJ: Enslow, 1993.

Kerrod, Robin. *The Environment.* Tarrytown, NY: Marshall Cavendish, 1993.

Landau, Elaine. *Environmental Groups: The Earth Savers.* Hillside, NJ: Enslow, 1993.

Lewis, Barbara A. *Kid's Guide to Social Action: How to Solve the Social Problems You Choose—and Turn Creative Thinking Into Positive Action.* Minneapolis, MN: Free Spirit, 1991.

———. *Kids with Courage: True Stories About Young People Making a Difference.* Minneapolis, MN: Free Spirit, 1992.

Lucas, Eileen. *Naturalists, Conservationists, and Environmentalists.* New York: Facts On File, 1994.

Markle, Sandra. *Kid's Earth Handbook.* New York: Atheneum, 1991.

Patent, Dorothy H. *Saving Wild Places.* Springfield, NJ: Enslow, 1993.

Pedersen, Anne. *Kid's Environment Book: What's Awry & Why.* Santa Fe, NM: John Muir, 1991.

Zeff, Robin L. *Environmental Action Groups.* New York: Chelsea, 1993.

Index